I0756251

FINISHING LINE PRESS
www.finishinglinepress.com

Milktooth

poems by

Caitlin Dunn

Finishing Line Press
Georgetown, Kentucky

Milktooth

ISBN 979-8-89990-481-3 First Edition

ACKNOWLEDGMENTS

I'd like to thank the following places for publishing the following poems:

The Poetry Lighthouse – "The Last Three Days We Spend in Italy;" "Eight Months After the Wildfire;" "At a Motel 6 on Interstate 40"
From Whispers to Roars – "Repeat"
Wingless Dreamer – "All the Sounds of the Benighted Wilderness;" "Rio Cucharas in Early June"
Canary Literary Magazine – "Zero Percent Containment"
Cozy Ink Press – "A Relationship in the Abstract"

Publisher: Leah Huete de Maines
Editor: Christen Kincaid
Cover Art: Carol Dunn
Author Photo: Caitlin Dunn
Cover Design: Elizabeth Maines McCleavy

Order online: www.finishinglinepress.com
also available on amazon.com

Author inquiries and mail orders:
Finishing Line Press
PO Box 1626
Georgetown, Kentucky 40324
USA

Contents

Part 1: Prescribed Burns

Zero Percent Containment

At seven, the raw
water cuts out. In the hills
before the sunset

we see where it went.
Fire in rebuking fingers
over Trinchera

Mountain and the Pass.
They say the sound of it is
like a coal train, or

a heavy North Wind,
but from the valley we just
hear helicopters

and ringneck doves. It
hasn't rained in months. Six hours
ago a man down

the way thought he'd strike
up a campfire to cook some
Jimmy Deans. The world
takes videos of
his last mistake while it crawls
like hate toward us.

A Relationship in the Abstract

unseeable junctions
like ultraviolets
nail our windows shut

you're too savvy to bite
through canvas
you already sewed up

but you abdicate
your place by me
as if a thousand cuts
was one too many:

my eyes are not dull

like a marionette
you're useless
without strings

you dream your hair
is feathers

and I pull them out
trying to lift you

Blue Eyes Penchant

I.
I don’t claim impatience
but

substitutions take precedence
while you wait for a change.
(This is my song, not yours—parallels are not commensurate). So.
While New York/LA/a home in Chicago

evolve to the more nebulous as our futures pry open,
you talk about the universe as if

it’s a seamstress and lie sleeping across the empty
canvas of your potential—

and, despite what you told me about
why your hands shake,
I only ever remember your eyes

are whiskey brown.

II.
Catastrophically,
we just don’t seem to work out.
The contingencies you
subscribe to
are metaphorical
(at least hypothetical), and I was bound to discover

I have your ex’s face and
name.
Maybe I’ll never ask
if you imagined us as a syzygy
or an Einstein-Chwolson ring—a conjunction
or just another flaw.

At a Motel 6 on Interstate 40

For Stella: I hope you come back

It's night in New Mexico. Halfway to Carlsbad,
you sleep under stars you can't see

through a popcorn ceiling. Air comes in
like heat, under a padlocked door,
facing west. In the lobby:

the smell of old chocolate,
the sight of heavy blow flies
like freckles on the wall. Long
fluorescent lights sing
up high like the dead.

You sleep stiff on a too-soft
pillow in a cold, starched bed.
The man beside you is not yours—

but then, nothing is.

Eight Months After the Wildfire

> *"The Spring Fire burning in southern Colorado is now the third-largest fire the state has ever seen… estimated at slightly more than 94,000 acres."*
>
> *—Denver 7 ABC report, July 2018*

A deep-voiced rainfall
river rolls up pasture like
a tongue on a reed,

playing past our white
headgates and over the marsh
where we'd put a box

of thistle-eating
flies. It pulls along opaque,
chocolate-dark ashes,

ten thousand parts per
million. Every crawfish,
trout, and minnow—gone.

Look at their bones lined
up, like bleached natural keys.
The waterbirds fly

south to the desert:
when the rain finally came,
it just carried death.

Part 2: Erosion

The Graduation Rate is Forty Percent

On Peachtree Street, we twist our capillaries
with high blood pressure until
some of them break,

pretend we're less miserable
studying without alcohol.

(We've been assured the greatest authors
never needed their addictions.)

Each character we write is
maladaptive, unmedicated,
so we promise by Gillespie Lake

one night in October
we'll never have children.

Senior year at 3AM, we sit in a conjoined
tile bathroom with the yellow lights on

and compare the bursts in our eyes
to flowers we won't have time to grow.

December 9, 2018, 11:49 PM

Re: The Spring Creek Fire

On the ground is hard
snow caked around rotting leaves,
draining from itself

like a cold sluice.
Since the wildfire, I can see
more snow on the peaks,

spliced clean to the dirt
where timber used to be. Wind
still smells like carbon,

and if it ever
gets warm again, I think the
river water will

run with tar. For now,
things sleep. What isn't frozen
is packed like mortar

between stones and ice.

Rio Cucharas in Early June

There is new land by the river, where a diversion
ate up the cutbank and flooded a red fox's den.

The wild is full of new mothers. On our farm:
ruby-throated hummingbirds, California poppies in the gravel.

As I drive up Mosca Pass, I see fields full of the easy
sleep of little cows, still wet from birth.

And I wonder how it feels to have air for the first time:
would that breath be sunlight,

or like drowning?

Necrarchy (Rule of the Dead)
—Re: "Decossackization"

at night, heat lightning
falls through clouds
like hands between bars

later it rains
heavy as a hailstorm
and worms come up to breathe in the dark

we are alone and
there are no eyes hunting me
still

I fear the highway, the river
lonely hawks and skinny lions
inside, *Dzhon Sirka's* moonshine jug
settles in the kitchen: ninety years back,

he'd hoped to take it home one day

at midnight, cleaning old crystal
I cut my hand holding

too tightly, and I ask my mother

through my teeth
when the blood will stop

at the kitchen sink,
water runs red from my palm   and disappears

Malathion 5

On the hill, there are
no locusts. No scrapesaw mandibles cutting into
grass, walking onions, or each other's wings.
In the August heat, I used

to find them turning on themselves like Ourobouros,
catch and handle them as if I could find
what made them sick.

There were birds here, too.
Blankets of starlings thrown lazily
down the mountainside, black-capped

grosbeaks bundled close to the ground,
hunting. We're lucky to see any, now.

We knew dead locusts would fill
the dry riverbed this summer.

We didn't know we would be alone, after.

What You Don't Know Will Hurt You

On hot chocolate days, I press
my fists to my eye sockets, look out the window
across the snow with glossy blindness,

wonder what will happen if you
catch me. Wrapped around myself
and tangled in blankets that smell like you,

I can't be hiding—
it's too obvious—but I hold
something in my mouth more than tastebuds

and teeth. I think it's a slow death
that keeps me here, breathing condensation
secrets into the glass. When I touch you,

I wish it wasn't because I fear
you've found me buried in white light
and decided not to hear me.

Adaptation

I.
Ravens trail us each day on Lake Powell.
We take handfuls of Swedish Fish from a crinkly bag
with sunscreen-greased fingers,

coconut and carnauba wax
an aftertaste like hundred degree heat.
Bluegill sleeping open-eyed

under the mooring,
the sun humming
in its deep blue mirage.

A hand-sized dragonfly wanders
into the cabin and we find it flying
against the kitchen window,

too full of instinct to retrace its steps.

II.
Above us is a vast, dark sky with lightning like the sun.
In a tent pitched on sandstone, we sleep to wake each night,

rising to meet the day. On the lakeshore in the morning,
we find old shells dissolving—becoming sand.
The years change us, too.

Visual Purple

On the first day at noon, my uncle
gives us flashlights with a red-glow
setting. We are young. We run off,
hand-in-hand.

When the sun abandons us, it's four-thirty.
The Escalante arm of Lake Powell,
winding stone, casts shadows a mile deep.

After hours in the barrens,
you and I use visual purple to
see across the sandstone. We climb
down, barefoot, from orange silica

still warm from the day. In cloudy water,
off the stern of the houseboat, we wash our hair.

Soon, we pull out blankets to sleep
on top deck, beneath Cassiopeia

for a little while.
In rhodopsin dark, the canyon
closes its hand.

Social Anhedonia

You're not home anymore.
You fled the state, joked
that only thieves and children

run. And you felt heavy.
But remember when you slept
in a new friend's car on the way

to the cinema in Pearl,
and your legs ached in the backseat
from walking all over campus?

When the last boy who kissed
you was cold and soft
and tasted like Blue Bell?

When you woke up rose-red
at midday in August,
as if the sun were holding you?

The last time you stayed up
all night, you thought you wanted
to keep the milktooth of your heart.

Maybe you were wrong.

Selective Sabbaths

I.
It's most of a day's
drive through the desert—double
yellow lines and no

one for miles. But then,
down a stretch that's six percent
grade, jog the brakes and

there's an oasis.
I saw it first at three or
four years old, all red

jagged cliffsides and
bitter-white aspen trees deep
in the canyon that

hides Calf Creek. Every
year we'd stay there in tents. When
it rained, the adults

took their Keystone with
water. When it didn't, they
threw cans in the fire

and watched them cave in.

II.
When I was little
my father could still carry
me on hikes. With my

eyes pointed down, I'd
press my white-blond hair to his
chest. Or sitting on

his shoulders, taller
than I'd ever grow, I'd tear
leaves from the high limbs

and keep them to burn.

III.
This place existed
before me. There were cattle
bones at rest in the

black mud before my
parents met there and wondered
if they could love each

other. I don't know
if the water remembers
who passes through. It

scattered my brother's
ashes twenty years ago
and swallowed them like

heavy sand. How would
it know my ankles and toes
from another's? Why

should a paradise
care about brand new bones when
it has so many?

Part 3: Ephemerals

Staying Inside from the Cold

There's a storm coming.
I wake up, 6 o'clock news,
with lungs full of fog.

My feet touch the tile,
mini-split A/C kicks on,
and I drive down south.

Out here, I can sleep
at night. Quiet slips over
me like a second

eyelid. Standing in
the valley, the nest I left

empty, I regress.

I'm a child again,
filling my pockets with small
riverbed jaspers,

hot to the touch and
unsocialized. Nothing is
a sound that constricts.

Day passes. The dogs
rest by the fireplace. It snows

outside until dark.

All the Sounds of the Benighted Wilderness

Sometimes she (or you) will dream
about the Mojave Desert and Joshua Tree,

from the summer of '02 or maybe

'04, when her parents owned
a thirdhand Jetstream trailer old

enough that she heard groaning

and knew it was ghosts. It was dry
there, and looking at the sun was like

eyes open in a blizzard. The yucca palms were wise

to it—they grew stocky and nettled
and shaded themselves better

than her family could, even under umbrellas

and the passing dark of tall rocks
as the sun came down. Her father's friends Ruth and Ross,

ancient as the early day, stopped

with them to play Scrabble in the little yellow kitchen
when the moon came out, and Ruth had brought bitter

lemon pie from home, and with arthritic shakes, she set it

by the sink for later. She couldn't spell like the rest
of them yet, so she listened for coyotes, desert kit foxes,

bobcats drinking the cold desert night, wherever they ran or
slept.

Repeat

I.
in Death Valley even shade was hot
where I could find it and the air
going fast was like standing behind
a truck's exhaust, breathing in

and there are shells there, on the sand hills
two hundred miles from the ocean,
white like dog's teeth and brittle

II.
in a ghost town, somewhere
near Buena Vista it is too high
up for mosquitoes and the river is clear
snowmelt, runoff, rapid, loud like wind

mountains are so still and maybe
older than snow, than the white pines
we call trash trees that bend for the light,
older than the sound of water
and some of the stars

III.
in the slope of the Natchez Trace
there is only a limb of sky
and it winds slow and gray
with fog like winter breath at night

and while I peel through
smaller than the bull thistles
a white-tailed deer behind the treeline
gives birth and there is no sound
at all but her breath

Hail in Southern Colorado

It's getting colder.
My mother feels it in her
joints. Hail clouds look like

bubble wrap mold-gray
when they're close, when they bundle
tightly to the ground.

My mother and I
draw some blue crinkly tarps
over lilies, phlox,

the bleeding hearts, hen
and chicks. My feet bare, I shoo
bee flies from the new

Russian sage. Pick rocks
to hold the tarp down. When the
wind comes it won't move

them. A mother and
child fold snap dragons to sleep,
the sky behind us

already aching.

Bitter Lemon, Butter and Eggs

I think I know, now:
not all yellow flowers are buttercups, not all

black birds are blackbirds. It's such a rare gift to see
clearly—to look for

the whiskers on catbirds,
not break even and call them *mimidae.* Most

of us give up when
we pry the Latin name out of them—my mother

says you can't *just* look.
The difference between toadflax and snapdragons

is in the close breath.

How to Forgive Yourself

It's here that I see you:
in summer, in red, through
haze from wild fire in the south,

and I think we must be
more than our blood
or the smoke we breathe.

I warned you once, I was built backwards and
barren. You only smiled
and said we've lived long enough.

In the end, we met on different
sun paths: we kissed each other's shadows
and slipped away. I love you, still.

But I wonder what would have
happened if you and I had stopped
watching the sky for

a moment and looked
at each other, decided that the fear couldn't stop us,
and we were old enough to know what we saw.

The Last Three Days We Spend in Italy

We are awake somewhere in Orvieto, in a garden
of red poppies, at dusk. I won't remember this. Then:
we cradle focaccia bread in paper
and skin blood oranges in Florence, stumble past
fountains of still water, miles of dark
cobblestone, a similar sun. I feel the same
in new languages and eyes
as I did at home—like paper torn poorly
from a notebook—

and I think we walk for days, heat above
and below us, my tongue
a heavy, dry stone. They found new ruins beneath Rome
last August. The excavation site wears
caution tape and beer bottles
like a chastity belt. I wonder aloud what it means
to dig up something so ancient, and you flash Dolomite
teeth when you say,
It's to admit you can't know
how anything ends.

With Thanks

For many reasons, for making the completion and writing of this chapbook possible, I would like to effusively thank my best friend, Grace Reeves; my boyfriend, Conagher Davis; my parents; my dear friends Morgan Johnson, Samuel McFatridge, Brandon Blanc, Azzy and Jay, Dillon Cannon, Molly Sample, and Marissa Martinez; my fellow writers (and also dear friends) including, but not limited to: Nicholas Olah, Micah Sample, Esso, and Alex Dawson; my writing communities on Instagram and at Lighthouse Writers Workshop; my college professors at Belhaven; my coworkers from ARC Thrift Store; and my neighbors on Mariposa Street. All of you have imprinted on my heart in more ways than you know.

Caitlin Dunn holds a BFA in Creative Writing from Belhaven University. Her work has placed in the Live Poets' Society of New Jersey poetry contest and the Southern Literary Award. In 2025, she was shortlisted for *The Poetry Lighthouse* Prize. She has been published by *The High Shelf Literary Journal, Canary Literary Journal, From Whispers to Roars, The Poetry Lighthouse*, and more.

Caitlin was raised in Southern Colorado, USA and currently lives in Denver, Colorado. Her hobbies include jewelry-making, photography, videography, and amateur entomology. You can find more of her work (poetry and otherwise) on Instagram @ *caitlindunnwrites.*

www.ingramcontent.com/pod-product-compliance
Lightning Source LLC
LaVergne TN
LVHW090540110826
845146LV00003B/1195

* 9 7 9 8 8 9 9 9 0 4 8 1 3 *